The Panda

Wild about Bamboo

text by Valérie Tracqui
photos by the BIOS Agency

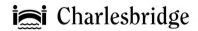
Charlesbridge

Library of Congress Cataloging-in-Publication Data
Tracqui, Valérie.
   [le panda, fou de bambous. English]
   The panda: wild about bamboo/text by Valérie Tracqui;
photographs by the BIOS agency.
     p.   cm.—(Animal close-ups)
   Includes bibliographical references (p. 28)
   Summary: Describes the physical characteristics, habitat,
behavior, and reproduction of the panda, one of the rarest animals
on earth, and discusses efforts to save it from extinction.
   ISBN 0-88106-737-7 (softcover)
   1. Giant Panda—Juvenile literature. [1. Giant panda.
2. Pandas. 3. Endangered species. 4. Wildlife conservation.]
I. BIOS agency. II. Title. III. Series.
QL737.C214T7313 1999   98-46101
599.789—dc21

The giant panda lives in bamboo forests high in the mountains of only six areas in central China.

Cloud country

The Chinese call the center of China "cloud country" because it rains almost all the time, and thick clouds hang over the mountains. Snow always covers the highest peaks.

High in a pine tree, a pair of golden monkeys chatter to each other as a snow leopard prowls through the dense, wet forest below. Loud barking echoes across the mountains, and a small whimper answers nearby. A large black-and-white animal pushes its way through a thicket of bamboo. It is the panda, one of the rarest mammals in the world.

A giant teddy bear

With its pudgy body and sad expression, the panda looks like a big, cuddly teddy bear. But though it seems slow and clumsy, it is incredibly strong and has terrifyingly sharp claws.

Thick fur, like armor, protects the panda from thorns. An oily liquid makes the fur totally waterproof, keeping the panda safe from the rain and cold.

An adult panda can weigh up to 350 pounds and measure five and a half feet tall when standing on its hind legs. The panda has weak eyesight, but it has very good hearing and often uses smell to communicate.

Thanks to its big paws and strong claws, the panda can climb trees easily. It comes down hind feet first.

The panda's jaws have to be very muscular to chew the plants it eats. Although the panda has 42 teeth like other members of the bear family, it mostly uses its strong molars to grind up hard bamboo shoots.

The panda has a long bone in each of its front paws that it uses like a thumb to grasp bamboo stalks.

The panda's black eye patches, ears, and leggings make it look like it is wearing camouflage. The black fur around its eyes protects them from the reflection of the sun.

In the summer the panda feeds mostly on the protein-rich leaves of the bamboo plant. During the rest of the year, it has to crunch the hard stems to get enough food.

The panda's stomach is designed to digest meat, and it cannot easily break down the hard fibers in bamboo. That is why the panda has to eat so much!

Wild about bamboo

At three o'clock in the morning, the panda is already hungry. Luckily a tasty thicket of bamboo is not far away. Before the panda can begin its breakfast, it must cut the thin bamboo branches with its teeth and tear the leaves off by sliding them between its fingers and false thumb. The panda then sits down, sniffs its prize, and peels off the bark to get at the crunchy, sweet center. It is hard work, and it can take all day before the panda is full.

An adult panda has to eat between twenty and eighty pounds of bamboo every day to get the energy it needs.

Because there is a lot of water in bamboo, the panda hardly ever needs to drink.

Disappearing food

Several bamboo species grow in the mountain forests of China. But sometimes all the bamboo of the same species flowers at the same time and then dies. It can take twenty years before enough bamboo grows back to feed a group of pandas again. The animals sometimes have to travel great distances before they find another place with bamboo.

Some species of bamboo grow up to half an inch wide and 16 feet high.

The panda sometimes eats other plants, insects, dead rodents, fish, and honey, but these are not enough to feed it when all the bamboo is gone.

A flowering bamboo plant looks like this.

Researchers find many pieces of bamboo where a panda stopped to eat.

The panda has to eat 3,000 bamboo shoots every day to get the nutrients it needs.

The panda eats bamboo even when it snows. It leaves scent traces using two glands hidden underneath its tail so that it can easily find its favorite meal spots.

Brr . . . it's cold!

Eating mostly bamboo, the panda cannot get fat, so it cannot hibernate like other bears. In the winter the panda moves down the mountain to warmer regions. Most of the time the panda lives in a small area between one and a half and two and a half square miles. It prefers to live alone and rarely shares its territory. Some pandas do not have a territory of their own, and they often wander great distances.

The panda communicates with eleven different sounds. It barks to say hello, and it growls, snorts, or gnashes its teeth if it is frightened. It may also leave scent markings as messages.

Snowy footsteps are the only sign that a panda was here.

Mating season

In April spring fever hits the mountains of central China. It is still cold, but the air already smells like tree sap and new bamboo. It is the panda mating season. Females rub against the trunks of pine trees to leave their strong scent on the bark. This special smell will attract all the male pandas in the surrounding area. It tells them that the females are ready to mate.

A panda couple only stays together for a short time.

Each female's mating period lasts only one or two days. She may mate with several males, but she will raise her babies by herself.

Males leave claw and tooth marks in the trees and scent on the rocks to show where they have been.

Mating season is the only time of year that pandas look for each other in the forest.

A loud roar fills the air when a male sees a possible mate. He barks, whines, and howls to attract her attention. But another male sees her too, and soon the two rivals are growling and clawing at each other. They roll on the ground, rear back up, and bite each other. In the end, the strongest wins.

Zookeepers built a wooden box for this mother panda and her baby.
Female pandas are able to raise a cub every two years.

A new arrival

The mother-to-be chooses a hollow tree and lines it with branches. Four and a half months later, a baby panda, called a cub, is born with its eyes tightly shut. It is mostly pink with only a little thin, white fur. It is barely six inches long and weighs only as much as a small orange!

The new mother holds her cub close to her own body, licks it, and changes its position at the tiniest cry. She will not leave her den for a whole week. But she is very watchful, and she will move to a new den immediately if she senses any danger.

The baby panda grows black-and-white fur when it is two weeks old.

So much to learn

At almost four months old, the cub still cannot walk. Its mother carries it from place to place by the skin of its neck. Often she leaves her cub in a tree while she eats so that it will be safe from predators. The cub sometimes waits for eight hours without anything to eat or drink.

In January the little panda takes its first steps in the snow. It quickly learns to climb up trees and crawl all over its mother.

The panda cub tastes bamboo for the first time when it is between nine and twelve months old. It also learns how to mark trees and recognize the scents other pandas leave behind.

When it is eight months old, the cub measures 32 inches long and weighs 55 pounds. Its soft baby fur has grown thicker.

Other plant eaters, like this sambar deer, are too rare to
compete with the panda for bamboo.

When the cub is full-grown, it will not be afraid of anything . . . except humans. It will be able to have babies of its own when it is five to seven years old, but it will have no more than six or seven babies in its lifetime.

Good-bye

The cub is now a year and a half old. It must leave its mother and join a group of other young pandas. They will travel together for a few months looking for new territory.

The new panda group needs a forest full of old, hollow pines to shelter pregnant females. The pandas want to find a place with several species of bamboo so that they will survive when one whole species flowers and then disappears. Unfortunately this kind of territory is becoming more and more rare. It could be a very long time before the pandas find a new home.

ForAll

Save the panda

Only about 1,000 pandas
survive today, and only 900
live in the wild. Their
territory continues to shrink
as Chinese farmers cut away
the forest. Poachers still kill
the panda for its valuable
skin. In 1980 the Chinese
government and the World
Wildlife Fund (WWF)
established a program to save
this worldwide symbol of
animal protection.

Once captured in a trap like this one, the panda falls asleep under
anesthetic. Scientists can then weigh and measure it.

Scientists put a radio collar around a panda's neck. They will learn a lot about the panda's living habits by using the signal
the collar sends to follow the panda's movements.

Every minute, a researcher takes notes about where the panda is and what it is doing. These activity charts teach him which territory needs to be protected.

Pandas are very good at hiding, but this researcher uses a directional antenna to find a panda wearing a radio collar.

A rescue plan

China is creating seventeen forested passageways linking fourteen new reserves filled with bamboo. In the Wolong reserve, specialists follow wild pandas to learn how to protect them.

In 1976 and again in 1983, some species of bamboo disappeared, and hundreds of pandas died. We have to find a way to avoid this kind of disaster if the bamboo disappears again.

Pandas in captivity

One of the ways to save pandas from extinction is to encourage them to have more babies and then release the young pandas into the wilderness. But pandas do not often reproduce in captivity, and protecting newborns is very difficult. Recently, of fifty-one pandas born in captivity, only nineteen survived more than two months.

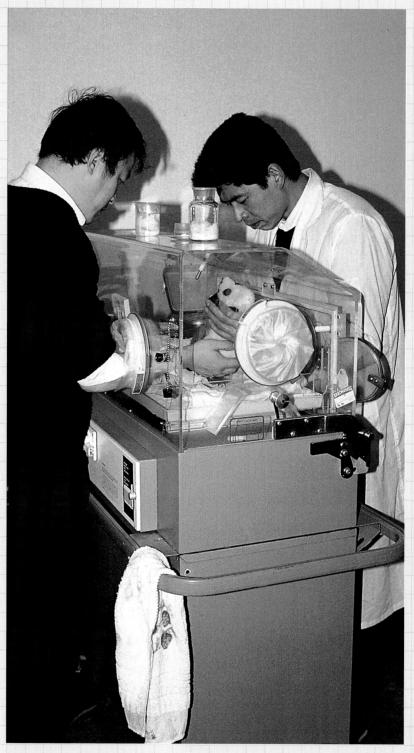

We must protect their habitat so that captive pandas will survive when they are released.

Immediately after birth, a baby panda is put in an incubator. It has to stay warm and safe from bacteria and germs.

It is very hard to bottle-feed a baby panda. Panda milk is not like the milk of any other mammal.

Artificial insemination

Scientists take sperm from a male panda and place it into the uterus of a female panda after she has been given anesthetic. This may make her conceive a baby. The first panda conceived this way was born in Beijing in 1978. Sometimes a panda gives birth to twins. When this happens, caretakers will usually take one of the cubs away and feed it with a bottle. In the wild, a panda mother tends to reject more than one cub.

With constant care from human helpers, a mother can sometimes be persuaded to take care of twins. They need her to teach them to communicate before they can be released in the wild.

25

Close cousins

A French missionary named Father David first told the West about the giant panda in 1869. Ever since, scientists have been unable to decide to which animal group the panda belongs. They finally decided to include it with the Ursidae, or bear family, even though the panda evolved differently from other bears a long time ago. Some scientists used to believe that the giant panda was part of the raccoon family like the red panda, the coati, and the kinkajou.

◀ The red panda, or lesser panda, eats bamboo and has a false opposable thumb just like the giant panda. Both species live in the high mountain forests of Asia. In addition to bamboo, the red panda eats baby birds, eggs, insects, and small rodents. It is about as big as a large cat and has thick red fur. It is called a panda, but it is not a bear.

The sloth bear lives in India and Sri Lanka. It has long, shaggy hair. The sloth bear likes to eat termites and ants. Babies often ride on their mothers' backs.

The moon bear, or Himalayan black bear, lives in the same area as the panda and is about the same size. But the moon bear eats many different plants and hibernates in the winter.

The Malay bear, or sun bear, weighs only 60 to 140 pounds. It lives in the forests of Malaysia, neighboring countries, and the Sunda Islands. The Malay bear eats both plants and meat. It does not hibernate because it lives in a warm climate.

For Further Reading on Pandas . . .

Arnold, Caroline. <u>Panda</u>. Morrow Jr. Books, 1992.

Kallen, Stuart A. <u>Giant Pandas</u>. Abdo & Daughters, 1998.

Presnall, Judith Janda. <u>The Giant Panda</u>. Lucent Books, 1998.

To See Pandas in Captivity . . .

Only three zoos in North America exhibit giant pandas:

The National Zoo, Washington, DC, U.S.A.   **http://www.si.edu/natzoo**
The San Diego Zoo, San Diego, CA, U.S.A.   **http://www.sandiegozoo.org**
The Chapultapec Zoo, Mexico City, Mexico   (no website available)

Use the Internet to Find Out More About Pandas and Other Rare Animals . . .

All About Pandas by Friends of the National Zoo
-Includes panda articles, an animated map showing the panda's decline, and a game.
    http://www.fonz.org/ppage.htm

Gander Academy's Panda Theme Page
-Includes resources for elementary students and teachers.
    http://www.stemnet.nf.ca/CITE/panda.htm

Pandas Pandas and More Pandas!
-Includes panda photos, pandacam, a game, and a resource page.
    http://www.geocities.com/rainforest/3019

See Updated Animal Close-Ups Internet Resources . . .
    http://www.charlesbridge.com

Photograph Credits

BIOS Agency:
Pu Tao: pp. 3, 4-5, 14 (right), 20-21, 25 (top); S. Zalewski: p. 6; G. Schulz: cover, p. 7 (top left); Jackson/WWF: p. 7 (top right); M. Gunther: p. 7 (bottom); H. Ausloos: p. 8; F. Polking/WWF: pp. 9 (bottom), 12 (bottom left), back cover; R. Seitre: pp. 9 (top), 27 (top right); G.B. Schaller/WWF: pp. 10-11, 23 (top); K. Schaller/WWF: p. 22 (bottom); Lenain: p. 10 (bottom left); T. Rautert/WWF: pp. 11 (top, middle, and bottom), 12-13, 22 (top), 23 (bottom); J.P. Sylvestre: p. 24 (left); S. Mainka/WWF: pp. 18 (bottom left),16,17,24 (right); Klein/Hubert: p. 26 (left); M. Harvey/Photonatura: p. 26 (right); D. Heuclin: p. 27 (top left); J.L. and F. Ziegler: p. 27 (bottom), Don Reid/WWF: pp. 13 (bottom right), 18-19; C. Ruoso: p. 15 (top); D. Halleux: p. 15 (bottom); T. Crocetta: p. 19 (bottom right).

Sipa Press Agency:
pp. 14 (right), 25 (bottom).

With sincere thanks to Francois Moutou, president of the French Society for the Study and Protection of Mammals, and to members of the WWF scientific committee for their scientific advice.